Read-About® Geography

Living on the Plains

By Allan Fowler

Consultant
Linda Cornwell, Coordinator of School Quality
and Professional Improvement
Indiana State Teachers Association

SCHOLASTIC INC.
New York Toronto London Auckland Sydney
Mexico City New Delhi Hong Kong Buenos Aires

Designer: Herman Adler Design Group

ISBN 0-516-24180-X

12 11 10 9 8 7 6 5 4 3   4 5 6 7 8/0

Printed in the U.S.A.   61

First Scholastic printing, January 2003

Long ago, glaciers, which are huge sheets of ice, moved over the land.

A glacier

The glaciers left many areas that are flat with few trees. This flat land is called a plain.

Some plains are not completely flat. They have low, rolling hills.

Rolling plains

A map of the plains areas of the United States and Canada

Plains cover much of the central United States and Canada. In the United States, the plains lie between two great mountain systems.

They are the Appalachian (a-puh-LAY-shun) in the east and the Rockies in the west.

The plains are split by the Mississippi River.

The part of the plains east of the Mississippi River is called the prairie.

West of the Mississippi, the plains are called the Great Plains.

Mississippi River

Bison

At one time, the only people who lived on the plains were American Indians. They shared the land with huge herds of bison, or buffalo.

Then great numbers of people began coming from the east. Many traveled in covered wagons, pulled by oxen or horses.

A family on a covered wagon

St. Louis, Missouri

The grassy plains became
a land of farms, towns,
and villages.

Some of the towns grew into
big cities, such as Chicago,
Illinois, St. Louis, Missouri,
and Topeka, Kansas.

Today, much of the plains is farmland.

The land is good for farming because the glaciers left rich soil.

Fields of wheat or corn spread out for miles.

A field of wheat

Machines like this one
gather the wheat crops.
You eat wheat in bread,
cereal, and pasta.

In some parts of the plains, there isn't enough rainfall for farming.

But the grass grows well enough for cows and sheep to eat. This is called grazing.

Sheep grazing

A farmer works his field using a plow pulled by two horses.

When farmers first moved to the plains, life was very hard.

Families had to grow all of their own food. Many made their own clothing.

Farmers worked their fields by hand. They often used horses to pull their plows.

Today a farm family's life is much different.

Machines like tractors make farming faster and easier.

People can get their food at grocery stores. They can buy their clothing at shopping malls.

A tractor

But life on the plains isn't always easy.

Winter days are often freezing. Summers are very hot.

Storms called tornadoes can destroy houses.

A tornado strikes a small town.

Despite difficulties, people who live on the plains have developed a way of life that is best for their surroundings.

Words You Know

bison

covered wagon

glacier

machinery

Mississippi River

plain

tornado

31

Index

About the Author

Allan Fowler is a freelance writer with a background in advertising. Born in New York, he now lives in Chicago and enjoys traveling.

Photo Credits

©:Archive Photos: 22 (DeWitt Historical Society), 13, 30 top right (Lambert); Dembinsky Photo Assoc.: 17 (Darrell Gulin), 21 (Emilio Mercado); Landslides Aerial Photography: 9, 14, 31 top (Alex S. MacLean); Photo Researchers: 25, 30 bottom right (Richard Hutchings), 3, 30 bottom left (Fred McConnaughey), 10, 30 top left (Tom McHugh), 5, 31 bottom left (Rod Planck), 18 (Earl Roberge); The Image Works: cover (Cameramann), 29 (Crandall); Tony Stone Images: 27, 31 bottom right (Alan R. Moller).

Map by Bob Italiano.